PRAISE FOR GLENNA MAGEAU

What Others are Saying about ***Do You Know Your Dad's Story? The Unasked Questions***

I have been eagerly awaiting Glenna Mageau's Do You Know Your Dad's Story? ever since Do You Know Your Mom's Story? was released, and the author does not disappoint... This book delves deep into a multitude of layers and stages, exploring everything from his childhood to what formed his beliefs in politics, religion and much more. It is also a time capsule, peeling back the years to reveal days gone past that cannot be authentically recreated in this modern day and age.

— P. M. TERRELL, AWARD-WINNING, INTERNATIONALLY ACCLAIMED AUTHOR OF HISTORY AND SUSPENSE

Well, I'm not really a sentimental guy but this got me and reminded me how much I don't know about my dad's story. Unfortunately, I can't ask him. I guess I need to make sure I share mine with my kids. Great idea. Wished I'd had this 15 years ago. He died too young.

— J. Z. (RETIRED)

By exploring our history we can learn so much for the future! The newest book from this award winning author is yet again, amazing. It's a great self-help tool to get to know our dads. It has all the right questions with enough variety so people can pick and choose what's right for them and their families. It's a wonderful way for adult sons and daughters to hopefully improve relationships with their Dad, learn something new or just have intriguing conversations with their fathers.

— CHRISTINE JACKSON (AUTHOR)

DO YOU KNOW YOUR DAD'S STORY?

THE UNASKED QUESTIONS

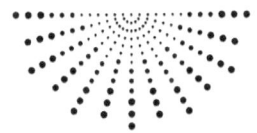

GLENNA MAGEAU

CONTENTS

Acknowledgments   ix
Your Dad's Information   xi
My Dad   xiii

1. Introduction   1
2. Understanding Dad   13
3. We Think We Know Our Dads   19
4. Being a Dad   23
5. The Time Your Dad Grew Up In   27
6. What is Your Relationship?   31
7. What is Your Dad's Love Language?   35
8. To Really Connect, Go Back in Time   41
9. How and When to Talk with Your Dad   45
10. Asking the Questions   51
11. The Fun Stuff   57
12. Your Dad's Birth   65
13. Upbringing   71
14. Family   79
15. School/Education   85
16. Marriage/Relationships   93
17. Career/Work/Jobs   101
18. Health   107
19. Wealth   115
20. Travel   119
21. Beliefs   125
22. Dreams/Aspirations/Goals   129
23. Favorite Things to Do: Hobbies, Sports, Music, Art, Writing, Dancing…   135
24. Raising You   141

25. Tough Times	155
26. Friends	161
27. Religion/Spirituality	165
28. Politics	169
29. The Most Helpful Things You Learned from Dad	173
30. Favorite How To's, Things He Fixed, Built...	181
31. Family History and Stories	187
32. Your Memories	191
33. Keep the Conversations Going	197
Dad	205
About the Author	207
Other Books by Glenna Mageau	209
More Books by Glenna Mageau	211
Thank You	213

First Edition: Published 2019

©Copyright Glenna Mageau 2019

All Rights Reserved.

Published by: Quadessence Press

Editing: J. G. H.

Formatting: J. Schlenker

Cover: Druscilla Morgan

ISBN: 9781775269847

All rights reserved. No part of this book may be reproduced or transmitted in any form or by any means, electronic or mechanical, including photocopying, recording, or by any information storage and retrieval system without the written permission of the author. Brief quotations embodied in articles, interviews, and reviews may be acceptable at the discretion of the author but acknowledgment must be given to the author. Thank you for respecting the hard work of this author.

ACKNOWLEDGMENTS

To all Dads, thank you for the role you chose to take on, it is not always easy, but it is full of gifts for you to reach out and embrace. Now it's time for you to share your story.
To my dad who was a hard-working man who didn't let his humor out enough but who taught me to work-hard, how to get things done and a love of nature.
To my family, Gerry, Jaz and Zack, you inspire me to take flight. Thank you. I love you.
To my siblings I am forever grateful for you. You are the best gift.
To my Beta Team – Christine, Sharol, Alisa, Helen, Jazmine, Zackary, Gerry, Patricia– your input is so incredibly appreciated and helpful. You are beautiful souls and I am grateful you are in my life.

To you my readers, you make my journey worth it. Thank you, I couldn't do this without you. To all of you, may you grow, mend and/or heal your relationship with your dad and may you have an amazing journey through learning about his life.

Your Dad's Information

Name:

Date of Birth:

Place of Birth:

His Parents:

His Siblings:

Where he fits in the lineup of siblings (1st, middle, last...):

My Dad

When I think of Dad, I think of strength

When I think of Dad, I think of hard work

When I think of Dad, I think of community

When I think of Dad, I think of adventure in nature

When I think of Dad, I think of a man with many talents

When I think of Dad, I think of a humor not often released

When I think of Dad, I think of games and sports and outdoor activities

When I think of Dad, I think of all I have learned and all I wished I had asked.

INTRODUCTION

Your dad has lived a full life and now it's time to discover his story. There are so many questions you'd probably like to ask your dad but you probably haven't had a chance or thought about taking the time to really get to know who this man is. I've given you a great way to get these conversations started.

My goal is to help you to connect with your dad in a new way. When you were a child, your dad was someone you looked up to—to be your protector, your guide, your mentor, your instructor. Sometimes he did it well and maybe sometimes he missed the mark. Sometimes you might have seen him a lot and sometimes hardly at all. You may have had a great relationship with your father or hardly one at all.

In some ways, men and in particular Fathers, like to share and find it easy to talk about certain parts of their journey, their exploits, how they learned something… Unfortunately, they don't often share the personal stuff—the feelings, the tough things they've been through, those things that didn't go well for them, what it was really like during their childhood… If it can be turned into a story, they are more likely to tell it. Some men are okay with bragging about their exploits and some aren't. Some came from this position of 'do as I say and don't question me'. Some were all about teaching skills to their children. Some were all about their kids being seen and not heard. Some have parts of their lives that they won't discuss.

Thankfully, times are changing but it is still somewhat of an issue for many men to open up and talk about themselves on a personal level. It can be really difficult, especially for older men, to really go back and share those things from their younger years.

Males, especially going back in history, have been seen as the tough, hard-working person, responsible for doing the physical labor. Men were expected to work hard. And Dads even more so. They had to be strong, show that they could be the 'breadwinner' and do all the hard, physical labor that needed to be done and look after the important things (i.e. financial). Their responsibility was to look after their family—feed, clothe and shelter them—and all that encompassed. Dads often had to work a lot. Some were farmers, some ran businesses, while others were the laborers. Some Fathers did really well at ensuring there was enough money to look after all the family needs but some really struggled with it. Times throughout the past have in some ways been much harsher for men and in other ways much easier. The expectations of men being the sole 'breadwinner' and responsible for the family is the expectation many Fathers were raised with. The further you go back in the time, the more prevalent it is.

The sad truth is that Dads, especially older Dads, didn't get much of an opportunity to spend time with the family as a family. They had too much to do, and they weren't often taught how to relate to or be a part of their kids every day lives. If they did find time to spend with their family, they might have struggled with leaving the harsh demands and expectations of life behind.

It's not whether we now see it as right or wrong, it's just what was. Times are changing and have changed a lot but there is still some of that expectation that men will take care of the physical needs of the family. Women have taken on a lot of that responsibility as well and thankfully are learning to give up some of their other roles—caregiver, nurturer, cook, cleaner... The responsibilities within a family are becoming more evenly distributed. At least to some degree.

The times were very different in the early 1900s to the mid 1900s to the present. The changes have been quite drastic in what we have access to, how we do things and to the thoughts and beliefs about gender and roles. What is acceptable today was not even discussed 20 years ago, never mind 30, 40, 80, or 90 years ago.

The role of dads has changed a lot over the last century. Dads are now more involved in all aspects of raising their kids but that wasn't always the case. For a long time, Dads weren't really involved in the day-to-day aspects of their child's life—from their home life, raising them, to what they did at school, to that of attending their children's events or activities.

When we reach old age, we should be happy, healthy, loving life, know that we made a positive difference, know we matter and to feel connected. If possible, let's do that for our dads, if you can't heal that relationship for whatever reason, then heal it from your perspective. Our relationships with our dads affect our lives in ways that we can't often measure, so the more we are at peace with that relationship, the healthier and happier we will be.

Being a Dad, I'm sure, is the most incredible gift and best role in the world but not always the easiest. Dads had to be strong going out in the world. Why? Because times were tough, expectations were tough, and the work was tough, but they also had to be leaders, providers and guides. Not easy to go from being this tough person, who is doing a lot of manual labor or running a business and often doing volunteer work in the community, and then come home and be present for his family.

Dads often have a more difficult time talking about their feelings than I think moms did or do. Especially the older moms and dads. Men were expected to do and be tough and hard-working and not complain or show emotion, especially for those things did not help feed, clothe or shelter the family. The problem is that we are emotional beings and when we stuff our emotions, we truly can only do it for so long. Anger tends to be the result. Unfortunately, one of the few places that it became the norm to express anger was at home. Sadly, this may have given you a really different view of your father and may have shown you a man who was very different in public than he did at home.

Did older Dads get to experience raising children the way they would have wanted? I don't think they really did get the opportunity. Not that older Moms really did either. The focus of the times was very different. There just wasn't really a lot of time or I would imagine energy, to spend time connecting with their kids. It was about looking after the physical needs. The physical needs were the big concern, the mental and emotional weren't really a consideration. Dads worked hard to provide for you, it was the expectation.

Our Dads are no different than we are but the times were very different—men had certain expectations and roles they had to fulfill. They had to show up in a certain way. Many older men are learning or have discovered their softer side, they are learning to hug and say 'I love you'. Sadly, it is something that was not done and not really acceptable 20, 30, or 40 plus years ago.

This book is so anyone who has a Dad can have the conversation with him about his life. To take the time to learn who he was, who he is, what he has seen along the way, his hopes and dreams, his frustrations, his struggles, what had real meaning for him, what did he want most for you... and so much more. It really is an in depth set of questions that will help you to document his story.

This book and the questions are geared towards those Dad's who are in their 70s, 80s, 90s, 100s... but it will work for capturing your dad's journey, no matter his age.

What really inspired this book was that I had written and published—Do You Know Your Mom's Story? 365 Questions You Need to Ask Her—and of course I immediately got requests for a book about learning Dad's story. It was also inspired by the fact, I don't know a lot about my dad's youth. He never really shared a lot and now I can't ask him. There are things I think of almost every day I would love the opportunity to sit down and talk to him about his childhood, about the times he grew up in, what his dream in life really was... Unfortunately, I'll never know those answers. Too often we just assume our parents will always be there.

The inspiration for this book also came about because of many conversations I've had with the elderly. I started out my career working as a Recreation Therapist in a nursing home. I met some incredible seniors and loved to hear about their lives. The one thing that saddened me, though, was many of these men often did not have great relationships with their families. There seemed to be a disconnect. When their children were growing up, they were busy working and trying to provide for their family. And it really wasn't an expectation for them to be there spending much time with their kids. It's just the way things were.

I got to meet these men as older men. I did not know them when they were young. I did not know them as fathers or husbands. I got to know them when the stress of being the man in the family, the father was no longer sitting on their shoulders. I got to know the softer, social side of these men. Something I would love for all families to experience but I know it isn't easy letting go of the past and the way you were raised.

Many of these men were looking to tell their story, what they had been through but did not feel they could share too much about their journey with their children. Some felt shame, some told me their kids wouldn't understand and some were worried about being judged. In some cases, they felt the family wouldn't be interested and for some there they had to still be the tough, protective man. Many of their journeys were never shared; this information, this life, this story was lost. The connection and understanding of who their dad was would never be discovered by the family.

Our dads grew up in a different time and if your dad is

elderly, the chances that he was either in the war or directly affected by the war are very good. He would have seen some ugliness, he would have seen food rations, he would have seen scarcity and he would have seen a lot of fear, heartache and pain. The effects of the war don't just last until the war is over, they are far reaching for years and generations to follow.

We all want to know that we matter in life, unfortunately, too many seniors don't feel this way. My goal is to try to mend, heal and grow the relationship you have with your dad so that you can understand him, see him and to help him to have some connected, fulfilled days, weeks, months, years, before he leaves this world. And so that we can too.

If you can't heal that relationship because of some things that can't be healed within your relationship or because maybe your dad just doesn't know how to, then at least you can heal yourself. This way when you reach old age, you will know that you have mattered, you can be happy, you can know you've made a positive difference and you can feel connected.

Being a Dad is an incredible role, but it isn't an easy one and it's often thankless. It truly has its own rewards but as a Dad if you aren't taught to look for them and are only taught to measure your worth by that of how your children show up in the world, then it is difficult to shift.

I truly hope you make the opportunity to ask your dad these questions while he is alive but if he has left this world, so you can't ask him directly, talk to other family members and some older people in your community who might know about his life. See what you can learn.

I think in some ways we are intimidated by our dads. We're intimidated in asking them about their lives. Many of us grew up with the understanding that what he said was to be followed without question. So now having that conversation with him, about his life, might seem a bit difficult. But know that he has changed, possibly a lot from when you were a child. He may be proud of some things he did with raising you and he may not be proud of other things he did with raising you. He did what he knew.

If having this conversation with your dad just isn't possible for whatever reason, still try to get to know and understand him. Know that the way he showed up was not about you, it was about what he'd been taught, the expectations put on him and how he had been treated. It does not excuse any bad behaviour but hopefully it will help you to understand him on a different level. It will help you to heal and to learn to forgive even if you can't mend the relationship. At least you will know that you can approach old age differently than your dad did. You can know that you mattered, you can be happy, you can know you've made a positive difference and you can feel loved and connected.

I've included a lot of questions, but it is by no means a comprehensive list. Choose the ones you feel are applicable and see what you can learn. They are in no particular order, so start where you feel works for you. This is a beginning to help you get the conversation started. There are so many things you will discover you can ask your dad and when he gets talking, keep asking and keep taking notes. Another option is to record your conversations. Just make sure your dad is okay with that. You could have the recordings typed up for you. Also, if you have a few siblings, you might want to talk to each other and try to coordinate getting this information so that you get it all documented. This will help to keep your dad from feeling overwhelmed with repeating the same stories. However, the truth is each of you may also get different information from your dad, from the same questions. Talk to each other and share what you've learned so you all can get a more complete understanding of this man, your dad.

After each conversation with your dad, be sure to reflect on all he has shared with you. And before you start the next conversation with him, reflect on what you've learned, what you remember and what you'd like to learn. Make this a positive experience for both of you.

Go into this quest with the understanding this isn't about you. Some of what you hear and some of the stories shared with you may surprise you, may make you laugh but some might hurt and make you feel unloved, unwelcome. Remember this is his journey, and he is sharing what he knows with how he knows to share it. Do not take any of it personally. All he tells you and shares with you or decides not to share with you is from a man who did what he knew, with what he had, in a time when he had a lot of specific expectations and responsibilities on his shoulders. It was his role and responsibility to look after the family. Let him have his moment, see it with love and understanding and humor. Discover the journey he has been on and all he has learned. It truly is worth it.

Enjoy your journey of getting to know this man, your father.

2

UNDERSTANDING DAD

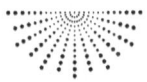

*D*ads come in all shapes and sizes, beliefs, abilities, skills, knowledge... some became Dads because they wanted to and some reluctantly. Some really embraced it while others ran from it. Regardless of how or why he became a Father, he really did want things to be better for you.

Often when we think of Dad, we think strong and dependable... they jump into a role trying to do it like how they do everything, with brute strength. He's trying to figure out who he is, how to raise his kids to be respectful, law-abiding, hard-working individuals, while providing all the necessities of life. It cannot be easy. There becomes an expectation that dad will always provide what is needed.

As kids we often just see him as Dad; that man in our life

who guided us, who pushed us, who scolded us, who tried to teach us, who's goal was to raise responsible, respectable children. He did what he knew with what he had. As his children we often don't see Dad as quite human, often we see him as bigger than life and forget that he may have had dreams and desires of his own and may still have. Do you know what they were? Or are? He may or may not have gone for them, but he may have been too busy working hard to make sure that the needs of the family were being met or he may not have had access to the money to follow his dream.

We also forget that he grew up in a different time than us. Just imagine all that you question, all that you feel is confusing and has put you in that place of not feeling you were good enough (cause we all do it) and go back in time to when your dad was growing up. There was little information out there, there was a very different mindset about men—what they should and shouldn't be doing and how they should be doing it. There were definitely different rules for men, different expectations and often the belief that the man was the one in charge, no matter what. It was a time when men really didn't share their thoughts, their ideas and definitely not their emotions, except maybe anger. They were seen as the one who dictated what happened in the family and how it happened. So think about the good and the bad that you learned from your dad and go back to when he was a child, guess who he learned from...? His dad grew up in a time of even more harsh expectations and more of a demand to be tough and to do the hard labor that was needed to be done—from building and heating a home, to clothing and feeding his family.

Understand that your dad's childhood, his teen years, his young adult life was a big part of developing his beliefs, habits and actions... a time that was very different to now. A time that was very different to when you were born. That's why it is so important to get to know him and understand him from that time he grew up.

What was he taught? What were the expectations?

What did he really want? Or did he even have a choice?

Time to step away from the role of Child and Dad and get to know this stranger who has been a part of your life... for a very long time.

Truthfully, there are about a million questions we need to ask our dads but often we don't because we don't think we can. I think that it has been really difficult for dads to share their lives with their children. They tell us a lot in their lifetime but how much is really about them? Do we really understand from his perspective or take the time to really get to know what he meant? How often do we really ask about his life as a child? About his journey before you were born to when he became your father? About the expectations of men?

Did you ever find that now and then he'd do something that would surprise you? It seemed so out of character for him?

Our dads often teach us things, everything from manners, to how to build things, to how to be responsible and work hard. We think we know our dads. We think we're pretty clear on who they are and what they want in life. But do we really know them? Do we really ask the questions of their life and how they lived, the ones that matter? Do we listen? I know we hear them even though dads would say we probably didn't. Too often maybe we brush off what they say as repetitive or really not all that interesting or as a put down. Or we listen but soon forget a lot of it.

It all depends at what age we ask all of those questions as well. As a child we saw our dads in certain ways—the provider, the discipliner, the one who demanded we do our chores, the one who showed us and told us to toughen up, the one who demanded respect, the one who wanted us to work hard... As a teenager we saw our dads as our guide, the buffer from life, the one we blamed for..., the one we avoided, the one we didn't talk to...

We didn't always respect him, but we did expect him to be there and to provide for us. As a young adult, we were often out to prove we knew what we're doing and that we didn't need help, at least not his help. We only asked questions when we really didn't understand something.

Dads were often sought out to fix something, to build something, to teach a sport, to ask something technical... No matter our age we are always looking to see if he's the role model we want to follow or not. Or one that we've got something to prove to. Whichever it is, we are always looking for his approval. There is a part of us that needs to know we have his nod that we're doing okay. And of course, we are always looking for his love.

3
WE THINK WE KNOW OUR DADS

We think we know our dads. We think we're pretty clear on who they are and what they want in life. But do we really? Do we really ask the questions of their life and how they lived, the ones that matter? And the biggest thing is do we listen? Sometimes they will talk about their journey and sometimes we listen and other times we sort of listen. Too often we may brush it off as repetitive or really not interesting or we see it as a putdown, that we're being judged. Or we listen but soon forget a lot of it. It all depends at what age we ask all of those questions as well.

Dads were often a little bit or a lot feared. They tended to be the authority in the family. When they said do something, it was often said with force and it was meant to be followed. Or there could be consequences. There wasn't really time for heart-to-hearts or explanations, it was a time of doing as he said. In some cases, Dads were avoided as you didn't want to be yelled at or told to go and do something. Too often they were seen as the disciplinarian, the one whose rules you had to follow. A Father's role was to be the one to keep the family in-line, everyone doing their part, and be responsible for having hard-working, respectful kids. In some respects, that meant Dads had to keep themselves separate from their children.

However you see your dad, my guess is that you may not have really had a heart to heart with him about him—his life... his dreams... his aspirations... the things that went well... the things that didn't... how he handled the good and the bad... his proudest moment... his saddest moment... his beliefs about himself... his beliefs about life... what made him happy... what made him sad... does he have regrets... is there anything he'd do differently if he had the chance... his biggest life lesson... what would he like to do differently...

Sometimes we've had these conversations where we've gotten some of this story. Sometimes it is because of a situation that has triggered a memory but too often we assume too much. We don't really probe or really take it all in. And sometimes he just won't share. Sometimes it's because he doesn't see it as important... or because he feels as though he did what he could... or maybe because he doesn't feel he has done enough... or he doesn't feel he needs to explain or share about his life...

Having a conversation with your dad can be difficult, especially if there is frustration, anger and past hurts underlying your relationship.

It can be tough to have this talk with him but it is important to start. Going through this book and getting the answers to his life will be a gift to you and to him but know that it is not meant to be done all at once. It might be too overwhelming for him and for you. This is your opportunity to connect with him on a different level. When you get into this, you will hear some stuff you've heard before but you may hear some new information. You may also hear things you want to hear but you might hear some things you don't. The best advice I can give you, don't take any of it personally or as a judgement against you. Just listen, ask questions, probe when he answers but stay out of your own stuff and do not judge him. He made decisions based on what he knew and what was available to him.

Finding out about his journey is about discovering who he really is, how he saw the world as a young child to that of where he's at now. The greatest gift you can give him is to not judge, nor get upset but to understand and accept. And remember he is going back in time so the way he is telling the story, what he remembers or what he thinks he might have wanted at a certain age, may have changed. He may also not share everything with you. Some things might be too hard for him to talk about, some he may not have a clue how to, some he may not feel he has to it's just the way it was and some he may have suppressed long enough he won't remember.

The key to this is to start the conversations that will open up the doors to discovering this man who is your father.

4
BEING A DAD

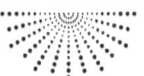

Your dad is that person that you love and sometimes push away. Sometimes seek for help, sometimes don't want any advice from. In fact, you'd often do the opposite of what he said. And as a dad you're expected to know what to do, when to do it and how to do it... no matter what. But let's be honest we are all doing what we can with what we know. Our dads were no different but most of them did it in a time when things were very different. There were very few books on the subject of raising children and it wasn't really something dads would have sought out to read although they might have written about it.

Love him. He may not have done everything perfectly or even well but he did what he knew. I'm pretty sure that every father's goal is for us to have a better life than he did and just about everything he has done has been to achieve that. Sometimes it might have been clear to you and other times you may not feel that is the truth at all. I do know that we hold Dads to a whole different level. I just want you to understand the human that he is—understand who he is, what he has done, what he wanted to do and why he made decisions that he did. Remember he has lived in a time very different than you.

Our dad's lived in kind of an awkward time. Raising kids in the 50s, 60s 70s had to be a bit difficult or at least confusing. It was a time of change. Roles were changing. Everyone seemed tired of the unwritten rules, the societal expectations, and the shut down way of being, especially for women and were trying to make changes to that. Even with all the strides to break free of the old—the old rules, the old manners, the old thoughts about women and their role—the old ways of being, still carried forward into a lot of what we were taught as children. This wasn't just a big change for women it was a big time of change for men. It was time to shake off the tough role, the strong role and start accepting that women had a mind of their own and were going to use it and were going to work right alongside men.

Women were changing their roles, so what did that mean for the men? Truly for a long time, Dads weren't often home for a good part of the day, so never really knew what work happened at home. Dad got up, went to work, did his work, came home and had food on the table, clothes washed and cleaned. With women starting to step outside of that traditional role of being the caretaker, it had to be a bit confusing and something that was very different than what men were used to. Of course, the concern would have been, how would everything be taken care of at home, in particular the children? There were in fact many men who supported the change for women. But wanting change and accepting the shift in roles can't always have been easy.

As we go forward in time, roles for men are changing drastically. Women are giving up a lot of the roles they felt they had to do and men are picking up many of those roles—they cook, clean, take the kids to school, stay home with the kids, look after the kids when they are sick ..

We are now in a time of rapid change, more so than at any other time in history. We are also in a time where pretty much everything is shared, is out there to be discussed. Well when your dad was growing up that wasn't the case. Many things weren't talked about openly and there is no denying that history has put men in a category all their own. They often could do what they wanted without too many reprisals or need for explanation.

Your dad has done and gone through a lot in his lifetime, learn what it is. For many of the older dads, I think it has been a lonely journey because men did not share their struggles, their questions, their feelings and still to this day, often struggle with this. That would have been seen as a big weakness and I think to some extent still is.

Your dad is amazing... but not perfect. Change the conversations you have with him. Let him know that he is important to you on a different level. That you want to know who he is. Also, by helping him to look at his life and the positives of his life, you just might help him to realize the gift he is. And you might learn a lot about who you are.

Men are strong, smart, funny and amazing workers but often forget that they are not on this journey alone. It's time to get Dad to talk about his life, his journey.

Ask these questions over time. And ask them again and again. Each time you might learn something new, a new memory will come to mind for your dad. Some of these questions will apply and some won't, and some your dad just might not want to answer or maybe can't remember.

Have fun with this but do get to know the journey that your father has been on. I want you to gather as much of that golden information about your dad as you can and preserve it for life. With this you'll always have that guide, that information that one day you just won't be able to ask him any more. Believe me that is the toughest day when you realize you can no longer ask your dad for advice on how to fix something or how to build something, who is so and so, how did he make..., just to talk to him...

Honor your dad, he is worth it.

5

THE TIME YOUR DAD GREW UP IN

*L*et me take you back in time. Your dad grew up in a very boisterous generation for men, especially if he grew up before the 60s. The mentality, the lifestyle, the beliefs, and the knowledge were very different than it is now. Men were really taught to be the one to ensure the family was taken care of and to work long hours if needed, to make that happen and that they pretty much had freedom of choice. Often dads were out of the house for long hours during the day but what they said was the rule of the house.

It was also in a time when things were becoming automated but lots still had to be done by hand—from heating the house, to the tools used for building things, to how things were fixed...—it was a lot of work. The man's role was to fix what needed to be fixed. For the most part because of his long hours of work, when he was home, he often had many chores/work/repairs to do. His work and life expectations often kept him apart from the family. If he was spending time with family, it was quiet time for him, or it was a time he'd teach some skill or on some occasions it was to have some relaxing, fun time together.

The truth is no matter what kind of life men lived back when your dad was raised, there was a real work-hard expectation for men. It was also a time when men didn't verbally express emotions. They did however often act out their anger and frustration. It would have been very hard not to adopt that kind of response, when it was really the only outlet for them. So what did that mean for your dad? It meant he learned he had to shut down his emotions and if he really wanted to do well; he had to work hard and take care of his family and potentially that of the community as well. It meant he had to close off part of who he was, who he is, and he had to distance himself from his feelings. Why? Because they made him look weak and really served no purpose. At least that's how emotions seemed to have been perceived. There was a lot of work to be done and feeling sad or lonely just got in the way. Emotions were something that weren't expressed a lot, at least not sadness. Even laughter seemed to be limited, at least at home.

You have this man, who is no different than you, he wants to know that he has done his best and is appreciated. To be strong, he had to take whatever came at him and keep going.

He had to show he could take it all on, fix it, mend it, deal with it and move on. When he got married and had kids, he had to make sure his kids understood the importance of manners and how to show up in public—image was very important. It measured how good you were. He was never hard on you because he didn't like you, but he had to make sure you learned the 'rules' because that also meant he was doing the right thing and doing what was expected and raising you properly. Unfortunately for the kids, it often translated into not being enough, not being good enough, not being worthy... Hence the yearning for Dad's love, Dad's acceptance and Dad's respect.

Don't get me wrong there were several dads who got this right, who knew how to say I love you, how to give a hug, how to be gentle and caring but there were those who did not. They tried to play by the rules, they tried to find themselves and maybe they tried to change the rules but got lost in what all that meant. And many of these men got lost in their roles and the expectations of how they were supposed to show up and all they were supposed to shoulder. And they had no one to talk to about it. You did not share you were feeling lost or not enough. Although I'm not sure that many men could articulate this, I think they just felt a lot of pressure and responsibility to be better. Besides, no one wanted to hear it. It was considered self-pity and there was no time for that stuff.

I think that many older men almost lived two lives—their public life and their private life. For many, they had one image they wanted the public to see but in private they could be who they were but this might have been overshadowed by them being so stressed by their public image that their private image wasn't all that nice. It could be confusing as to why this man was one way with others and than very different at home. This is where too often as a kid you might have thought you were doing some wrong, that there was something wrong with you, when really you had nothing to do with it. He was just trying to cope and to follow the societal norms that were set out for him.

What does it mean for you in trying to build a relationship with this man who raised you? It means you need to understand where he was coming from when you were little and where he's at now.

6
WHAT IS YOUR RELATIONSHIP?

*C*onnecting with your dad is one of the most rewarding gifts but can also be the most difficult thing to do. It all depends on your relationship with him. If you were/are fortunate to have a loving, giving, open and receiving relationship with your dad be sure to treasure it because it is a type of relationship a lot of people did not and do not have.

Many adult children just accept the relationship with Dad as is without realizing it can be changed. Too often as adult children we believe we have tried to connect, to get his love, to get his approval, but he stays the same. And he very likely will but... you can change. Before you get mad and think, I'm always the one trying to do things to make it work, there are a few tips that might help with altering your relationship. How you approach your dad can make all the difference. Too often we come from where we are at, from what we know and believe today, and can't figure out how come he can't show his emotions more or why he can't change his attitude. The truth is that in many cases if he had, he wouldn't have made it to the age he is and he might not have survived all he went through.

Your relationship with your dad falls into at least one of these categories, depending on the situation and sometimes the day:

1. A loving, mutually respectful relationship
2. A friend-type relationship
3. An intellectual relationship—you have good conversations but not personal ones
4. An emotional relationship—more of a push and pull
5. A superficial relationship—you talk about the weather, the neighbors...
6. Barely speaking—more of an avoidance relationship, you don't share personal information, if at all possible
7. Not speaking

It doesn't matter how old you are—6 or 65—there is this need to feel loved, accepted, respected and have your dad's approval. It is something all children strive for. It's kind of an odd feeling when you are a mature, independent adult and you realize you still have that yearning, that need. It is normal though and really shows how important it is to a child, no matter their age. Sometimes you know you have love and acceptance from your dad. Or you feel you may be able to work towards getting it and having him show it to you. Or you may realize it just isn't going to happen because he can't. Which probably means he never got it. Whatever happens with your relationship, you need to come to peace with it... for your sake. Do what you can to heal it but also know, you are enough. You are a beautiful, smart, loved child. Your dad just might not have been or be able to show you... at least not in the way you need.

Remember he grew up in a very different time with different expectations, understandings and ways of expressing love or caring.

WHAT IS YOUR DAD'S LOVE LANGUAGE?

*T*hat seems like an easy enough question and the simple answer would be that he tells you, 'I love you', right? Unfortunately, it isn't always that clear. And with older dads, often didn't happen, they didn't say 'I love you', at least maybe not when you were a child, the time you needed to hear it the most.

I've talked about the fact that your dad grew up in a different time. He grew up in a time when emotions weren't really encouraged and neither was positive physical expression of touching—hugs, a pat on the back... He might not have said, 'I love you'. He may not have been one to talk to you much, other than to tell you to do your chores, do your homework... On occasion when you were little, he might have given you a piggyback ride or let you ride on his shoulders. I'm not going to get into all the reasons why you didn't hear or feel that love, but it was the norm in many cultures. And still is in some.

The truth is that your dad probably never heard 'I love you' from his parents or perhaps anyone. It just wasn't done.

Today, it is quite normal and natural to say, 'I love you' and to give a hug. Your dad might have even learned how to do that, which is awesome but if he didn't do these things when you were a kid does that mean he didn't love you?

Unfortunately, I think too often that's how we, the kids saw it. We often wondered and would look for those moments of praise, which could also be few and far between. It was more often than not, the lack of getting in trouble that was what was the key that we were on Dad's good side.

So how did Dad express his love? And believe me he did it in many ways. For many Dads, doing the manual things around the house—building things, fixing what was broken, making sure that there was heat, food, water, shelter, finding ways to lighten the workload if possible and improving things to work better—were the things he did that were his way of expressing his love.

Did your dad used to build things for you or for the family?

Did your dad fix up something for you to use?

Did your dad push you to work hard?

Did your dad get on your case about homework?

About chores?

Did your dad work extra hours, so you'd have money to buy a special pair of shoes? Or special clothes?

Attend a special event?

Did you always have heat? Food? Clothes? Or did he at least work hard towards providing that?

Did your dad make sure there was always enough food on the table?

It may not feel like that was love, but it was. It was his way of showing love and it was what was an accepted way of expressing emotion. For some reason it seemed that stating your feelings was seen as a weakness.

Think back to the little things he used to do with you.

Did he take you on hikes? Out in nature?

Did your dad teach you how to build something?

Did your dad teach you skills?

Did he take you to special places?

What were the little things he used to do either with you or for you?

Did he push you to try new things?

Did he teach you sports? Hobbies?

Did your dad plan some fun occasions?

Did your dad take you fishing? Hunting?

Did he teach you how to ride a bike? A horse? How to drive?

We don't tend to see those things as anything but what a Dad is supposed to do. He's supposed to do all of that. True but he also had to work very hard and long hours to make sure that you were taken care of. He didn't have many of the modern conveniences we have today. He was showing he cared for you in the best way he knew how and still be able to keep on top of everything.

Sometimes it's by the things he said... over... and over... that were his way of expressing feelings.

Not all Dads got it or get it right but I think most at least tried to. Know that your dad loved you. He may not have said it, he may not have been able to show it but he did. No matter what he may have said or done, he loved you. Just remember it was different times and how and when love was expressed is very different than today. However, it is still something that some Dads struggle with expressing, even today.

Sometimes he might have been trying to discover if he was loved. He may not have heard it in his lifetime from an adult, never mind his children. Moving forward, let him know you do love him. Tell him often 'I love you', help to teach him it is okay. You might just be amazed at how much it truly means to him and to you. If you truly can't do that because you just don't have that kind of relationship or the possibility of it, then imagine it happening. Imagine having that loving, giving moment and make it your truth about your relationship. Why? Because it will help to heal you and those old wounds, you might be carrying around.

If you are trying to connect with your dad today, try to approach him through the things he likes to do, to watch... But also try to show him the things that have meaning for you, just don't expect him to love what you are telling him or what you like. He has gotten to a stage in life where he is getting comfortable with his life and doesn't want a lot of change. Honor that, it doesn't mean you can't show him new stuff or give him new experiences just know he may not be interested in doing it again. It has nothing to do with you but with the fact he likes the calm, controlled world he's created and doesn't want to change it. He's finally got some peace in his life and doesn't feel the pressure to be the one to fix things.

Remember, going into old age is about being happy, healthy, loved and connected, and to do that you need to heal. His story is as much about you as it is about him.

8
TO REALLY CONNECT, GO BACK IN TIME

To connect to your dad, you need to go back in time, to his time, to when he grew up. It is when he is most connected to. Find those things that have meaning for him, those things he knows from when he was young and growing up. Start with generic things he can relate to—work, fixing things, transportation, community events... It might mean you need to learn some history—what was going on when he was a child, what were the conditions like, how did they heat their homes, how did they cook, where did they get their food, what did they get paid, how did they get around, what did they use for transportation, how did they do laundry, how did they communicate long distance, what was the community like, what was the weather like, what was school like, where did they get their clothes, what were the expectations of men (in his words), what was the political world like... No matter what generation he grew up in things have and do change very fast. Technology and all we do, how we do it and all we use, has changed a lot over the years.

Talk about the similarities and the differences in the times. What does he think about the progress? What does he miss from his old days?

Once you've started conversations, then get into more personal ones. What did he love to do as a child? What was it like growing up where he did? There are many questions in this book you can start asking him but know it's not just about getting his information down on paper, it is about understanding him and who he is and who he was. Some things have changed a lot for him and some not as much. What tends to be a bit slower in changing, is the attitude, beliefs and habits that we all carry forward. They get passed on from generation to generation. Each time we strive to do better and be better but although there are a lot of changes in our physical world, it takes longer for us to shift how we see, act and react to each other. So it might take him a while to understand that sharing his journey is a good thing.

Something you can do to start or to expand the conversation with your dad is to not only listen to his journey but to share some of your experiences and your story—your doubts, your worries, your issues... Share about yourself. Let him see some of your vulnerabilities, some of your struggles, some of your understandings about life. You might be reluctant as you might think he'll judge you and might say something that hurts you. If that is a concern, start the conversation with telling him you want to share with him, but you don't want a negative response from him. See how he reacts. And ask him, 'Did he want to connect to his dad but didn't know how?' If you get a positive reaction, try it. Start with telling him the easy stuff, the stuff that won't hurt if he knows it. If he does say something hurtful, you will know you can't go this route, at least not fully. Hopefully you will be able to get some discussion happening to where you can connect on a deeper, more personal level.

When you talk to him, go in with no expectations and an open mind. Talk to him like you would a stranger and use all those manners he taught you. It truly can be really eye-opening and a lot of fun. But if you are feeling some anxiety or worrying about old patterns, take a deep breath, and step out of your hurt, pain and frustration with him. If you hold on to all he didn't give you as a child, as a young adult, as an adult, you may not understand who he is and you may not mend this relationship. When I say mend, I mean from your perspective. These questions are but a tool to help you to get to know this man. Hopefully it will help you to come to some sort of peace with whom he is and how he raised you and the relationship you have or don't have.

There are many ways to approach talking with your dad and with getting his history, but you may have to be patient and nurturing. He may need to know you aren't going to take his information and judge him. Unfortunately, he may feel that way. It might be like your reluctance to share with him. He might be where you learned it from.

Think back to when you were young and how much things have changed from then to now. Add another 20 years or so to that and imagine all the changes your dad has seen in his lifetime. Change isn't something many of us tolerate well, so just think of the huge shift in everything you know from the growth in the size of the communities; to drastic changes in transportation; to the different styles of clothes; to the ways and opportunities to travel; technology; the cost of everything; to contacting and connecting with someone—cell phones, text messages, email; to social media—sharing everything that was kept private...

Things are miles apart from when he was a child.

9
HOW AND WHEN TO TALK WITH YOUR DAD

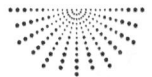

*D*eciding to talk to your dad is a big step, especially about his journey. It's kind of easy for us when we've gotten to that point that we want to hear about Dad's story but it is important to remember it might be an emotional roller coaster for him and for you.

Dads I think are more open to talk about their lives, at least the work, the physical part of their lives. Talking about emotions, feelings or the impact certain things had on others, might be a bit more difficult for him to do. And he may not want to talk about raising you. He may feel what he did was right and not to be questioned. He may feel guilt that he couldn't connect on a different level. He may feel that his job is over and he's not going back to it.

Men have a different view of the world and have had a

much easier and in some ways a much harder time. It has been easier to do the things they wanted to do, from work, to education, to activities, to voting, to having a say and being heard but it has been harder in that there have always been expectations that men be strong, tough and in some ways unquestionable. They were also meant to be the breadwinner and not to talk about their feelings, their struggles. They were always putting on a persona of knowing what they were doing. Men born in the early to mid 1900s really went through a lot of change in their lives—mostly that women were stepping outside the norm but there was war and unrest. So they have had to learn to adjust to the changes in times. Some have done well with this and were even a part of making those changes while others didn't know how to let go of the control and role they had.

When you want to sit down and ask your dad about his journey his life, make sure that you are gentle with him, start with those things that will get him talking. If you know of some areas of his life, he doesn't like sharing or you've seen him get mad when someone has mentioned a certain time in his life. Do not start there. Often asking where and when he was born is a good place to start, but it all depends on whether that is a traumatizing time or not.

Sometimes it is good to be direct and just tell him you'd like to learn about his journey, about who he is. However, for some men this is really tough to do. So you'd be better to wait until you are doing an activity or you're talking about something that you know might relate to his past. Then you can ask him how it was in his day.

For example, if you know he loves watching baseball, ask him questions.

Did you ever play ball? Where did you play? What got you started? How good were you? When was the last time you went to a game? Who did you play with? What age did you start? How far did you go with it? What is your fondest memory of playing ball? What was the best game you ever played?

The truth is that being a Dad is a journey. There was so much to do and to look after and no rule book on how you are to raise little ones, dependent on you. For most Dads, it really was about making sure the physical needs of the family were being met. Nowadays there is a shift in the expectations of Dads and their roles. Fathers are so much more involved in all aspects of a child's life. There is so much information for new Dads and support in helping them in this role. But think back to before the '80s, there was not a lot of information. Men weren't really expected to connect or have all that much to do with their children. They were often in the position of the authority and disciplinarian. The sad truth is that many Dads didn't get the opportunity or had the know-how to connect with their children. Not really on a personal level. They did try through teaching skills or taking the family on vacations or some other similar project. Men didn't ever talk with each other about raising their kids. It just wasn't a subject that was really broached unless of course they had a child they were having a lot of trouble with and it was public knowledge. Then they may not have had a choice as others might have wanted to give advice as to how they could get that child to do better.

Often your dad was not really involved with raising you and your siblings. Prior to having kids though this man had dreams and aspirations and ideas about where his life was going. Do you know what those were? Do you know how your dad felt about being a father?

This isn't about digging up dirt or finding a reason to get mad at your father but it is a way to get to know him and understand him a bit better.

There are so many things that happen in a lifetime but I truly believe that being born before the 70s you are seeing drastic changes in the world and in how things are done.

Do not ask all these questions at one time. Ask one, let him answer and then keep probing with another question.

If you're struggling to get him to talk about himself or his life, take him to some events he'd enjoy or to some place you know he likes or out for lunch and just ask casual questions. 'Did he have anything like this when he was a child?' or 'How did they do that when he was young?' Fit the conversation into the situation you are in. Really, he wants to share but he may not know how, so create opportunities for him that take the direct focus off of him.

The other thing you can do is to give him this book and ask him to go through the questions and to write out what he remembers about his life. He might find that easier to do. Be sure to ask him now and then though, about some memories he has written down. Try to get him to talk to you about it. Ask if you can read what he has written. He may let you, but he may not, so don't make a big deal out of it. Encourage him to keep writing, just understand it might be a cathartic journey or it could be a difficult one for him.

Today there is so much information for new Dads and support but think back to before the '70's, there was not a lot of sharing about how to raise your children. The unwritten rule seemed to be to raise quiet, hard-working, respectful young adults.

This could be a sensitive journey for your dad which might be why he's reluctant to share it. It may appear as if you are questioning how he raised you, something he may not be willing to discuss. Be there for him, understand him, give him the love and support he needs and let him know you understand. Take your time but find a way to talk to him, it will be worth it.

10
ASKING THE QUESTIONS

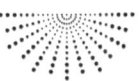

*A*sking the questions on the following pages will help you to get to know your dad and have a whole new understanding and appreciation for his life.

There are so many ways to approach talking with your father, from outright asking questions to doing it subtly as situations arise. When you have a conversation with him to start learning about his journey where you start will depend on three things:

1. the relationship you have with your dad;
2. how ready you are to hear some of it;
3. how ready your dad is to talk about it.

It is important to know there is information he may not

want to share with you. Be okay with it. Some things might be too difficult for him to discuss with you—privacy, guilt, shame, not feeling good enough, not wanting to hurt you or others, doesn't feel it would help anything, he doesn't see it as important... If he doesn't want to talk about a subject you can ask him why and he might tell you—he feels guilt... shame... it would hurt you... it's none of your business, but he may not. The purpose of this is not to offend him or to make him mad or to have him withdraw from you, so if he refuses to tell you anything, let it go. Just let him know that you don't judge him and only want to get to know him and his journey. Let him know that you understand and respect his decision but if he ever changes his mind, you'd love to hear about his life.

If he won't answer direct questions about his life or says, 'I don't want to talk about me', then wait until you're in a situation to bring it up in conversation and switch to asking general questions. If you can prepare for your time with him—and do some homework so you know some of the history of the time when he grew up, of the things that were happening, of the things he was involved in, the more you will be able to draw out of him.

"Dad did you ever get to drive as a kid? If yes, what did you drive? Where did you drive?"

"Who taught you how to drive? When did you get your licence? What kind of vehicle did you drive?"

"Dad, what was the first phone like that your family had? Was it a party line?"

"What was your first job? How did you get it?"

"Dad were you ever directly affected by civil unrest in the world?"

As I mentioned we all want to know we matter, if your dad is reluctant to talk about himself or his life, recognize it is a lifetime of learning that has him keeping quiet. The truth is you may have a difficult time getting him to talk but even if you only have superficial conversations about the weather always try to take it back to when he was young. You can ask things like, what was the worst storm he ever saw? What were they doing when it hit and how did they manage to get through it? You can learn a lot about his life through this.

The one big thing you can do for this man, whether you heal the relationship with him or not, or feel you aren't getting much from him, is to tell him you are grateful for him. Let him know you understand he had a lot to deal with and that it couldn't have been easy. To help him to see the positive, give some examples of some good things he did for you from when you were kids... teens... adult... Again, be prepared for any response from him because it might be a good one but it might not be. He may accept what you say and say thank you. Or he might not do more than not, he might not be able to show he is touched by it. Or he might acknowledge you've told him but not really express much. Or he may push it away and ignore it. Even though what you say is positive, he might not be able to accept that admiration. Know that he heard you, he just can't go there. Taking praise or being recognized for who he was and what he did are probably not something he was taught or has heard much, if at all. He really may not know how to respond. Emotions were something that probably didn't serve him well in his lifetime, so for him to start expressing them or to step back into sentiment or gratitude, might just not be possible. The truth is he probably hasn't learned how to say or react positively when he gets praise, so you can take this time to teach him. Simply tell him what you need from him, 'Dad, I need you to say thank you when I do this...', 'Dad, I'd really like if you'd stop saying...'. 'This is what I'd like to hear you say...'

Be gentle, be kind and do not take it personally if he is gruff or can't express what you ask. Just keep reminding him, gently. He is doing what he knows and just like the rest of us, he doesn't like change. He wants a life of peace and one where he is in his comfort zone. It might not be one you like or understand but it is where he feels safe and is in the most control. Recognize this, as it might help you to shift from seeing it as a slight against you.

Depending on your relationship with your father and where you are at with accepting your childhood, will depend on how you feel about talking with your father. It can be a bit more intimidating and difficult to talk with your dad about his life. At least to get the answers that you might be looking for. We all go through tough times in our life, the hard thing is being able to put them into perspective and move on without those things keeping us down and angry or bitter. The best piece of advice I can give is to come from gratitude. Be thankful of every day of every event but don't hold on to the anger. Look for the good, look for what you can learn and move on. If your dad is struggling help him see the good in his life, the positive that has come out of it.

I've laid out the questions so they are by topic but they are really in no particular order. Start where you feel you need to and with the questions that are relevant to your Dad's life. I've also provided some blank pages after each section for you to write down the stories he shares. There are more blank pages at the end of the book so that you can capture more of his information and memories.

This is your journal of your dad's life, enjoy the journey.

THE FUN STUFF

Too often we forget that our dads had a life before us, he had hopes and dreams and did things. It's time to find out a bit more about him. Let's get to know some of the fun stuff in his life. Getting him to share might be a little more difficult, although, generally I think he'll be more than happy to share the fun stuff. Some dads don't always see that they've had any fun or remember it, the tough times are often too prevalent. Ask though and be persistent in a nice and supportive way.

Did he ever do something daring? Or want to? Did he ever climb a tree?

What's the funnest thing he ever did?

Who was his first kiss? His first love?

What did he get in trouble for? How did that come about?

What was the best part of his childhood?

Who did he want to be when he was young?

What was his favorite song or music when younger?

What is his favorite song or music now?

What was his favorite book/story as a child? As an adult? Now?

What activities/sports did he enjoy as a child? Teen? 20s? 30s? 40s? 50s? 60s? 70s? 80s? 90s? 100's?

Which were his favorite?

Did he have a favorite toy as a child?

When did he learn to drive? Who taught him?

What would he change if he could go back in time?

What was the best part of being a dad?

What education did he get? Why did he take the level of education he did?

What kind of work did he do when young? How much did he get paid? What kind of work and what kind of hours did he have to work? What was his boss like?

Where does he believe he got his strength from over the years to deal with all that occurred in his life?

What is he most proud of?

What is something he always wanted to do or to learn but didn't?

What's an embarrassing moment in his life?

What are some of the fun events in his life? In his childhood? Teens? In his 20s? 30s? 40s? 50s? 60s? 70s? 80s? 90s?

Did he seek out fun things to do or if they happened, they happened?

Who did he have the most fun with?

What were things he saw as fun?

What made him laugh?

Did he enjoy laughing?

Did he laugh much?

Notes/Stories

Notes/Stories

Notes/Stories

Notes/Stories

YOUR DAD'S BIRTH

Birth is something that is magical, unexplainable and something that many fathers either weren't given the option to be present or they weren't interested. I think it's a bit scary for men when there is not much they can do but be present and be the support. Today, a father is much more likely to be present and involved in the delivery.

What is your Dad's full name?

What is his date of birth?

What time of the day was he born?

Where was he born? What town/city, province/state, country?

Where exactly was he born—in hospital, at home, enroute, other?

Was there anything unique about his birth?

Were there any complications with his birth?

How was his mother's pregnancy? Were there any issues, anything unique that happened during the pregnancy?

Who was there when he was born?

If he had siblings, how did they feel about having a new baby brother?

What has he been told about how he was as a baby?

Where did he sleep as a baby? (crib, dresser drawer, in bed with parents...)

What were the times like when he was born?

What was it like back in the times when his mom was pregnant? How was child-bearing viewed?

Something his dad had very little to do with?

What kind of medical/birthing support was there?

What was needed for him or his siblings when born?

Was his dad able to be present when he was born?

Was he interested in being present? Was he offered the option to be present?

Notes/Stories

Notes/Stories

Notes/Stories

13
UPBRINGING

What was his upbringing?

Understanding more about his background, where he was raised, how he was raised, the beliefs he was raised with, the rules, how his family interacted... all will help to give a better picture of him, his life and who he is.

Where did your dad grow up? In the country (rural)? In the city (urban)?

What is his favorite memory of growing up?

Did he have a nickname? How did he get it? Did he like it? Is he still called that? By whom?

What kind of things did he do as a child? By himself? With his siblings? With his parents?

Did they do family activities? What? How often?

Was there something they liked to do on a regular basis?

What is his least favorite memory of growing up?

Did he have to do chores? What chores? At what age did he start getting chores?

Was he close to his mom and dad? One more than the other?

Was he close to his siblings?

Did he ever get into trouble? What was he doing?

What happened? Did he ever do it again?

What did he spend a lot of his time doing? As a child? Tween? Teen?

What were things he liked to do that his parents disapproved of?

Did he ever hide things from his parents?

What does he think his parents wanted for his in life?

Does he still do any of the activities he learned while growing up? How long did he do some of them—only as a child, into his adult years? i.e. sports, music, creatively...

Who did he talk to about problems? As a child? As a tween? As a teen?

Did his family do things in the community? What? Where? How frequently?

How did his family celebrate special occasions—Holidays/Stats, Birthdays...?

Did they play games? Sports? Do other activities?

Was he from an artistic family? What kind of things did they do—painting, drawing, writing, hobbies, crafts, etc.?

Was he from an athletic family? What kind of sports/activities did he do? Did they do?

Did he feel he fit in with his family?

Did he feel his parents were there for him?

Did he feel his siblings were there for him?

Did he ever date? At what age did he start dating?

How did his parents feel about him dating? His siblings dating?

Who was his first love?

What would he change about his childhood if he could?

What is his biggest realization about raising you?

Your siblings?

What did he fear as a child? Why?

What was the house like that he grew up in?

What was it like in the neighborhood he grew up in?

Were there a lot of community events? What were they? Did they attend?

Did they ever go on a vacation as a family? If yes to where? How did they travel?

Notes/Stories

Notes/Stories

Notes/Stories

Notes/Stories

14
FAMILY

His Family
Parents, Their Siblings, Grandparents

*P*art of understanding your dad and getting to know more about him, is to get to know more about his parents, his grandparents, his aunts and uncles...

Who are your dad's parents (your grandparents)?

What is his dad's (your grandfather's) story—when and where born, upbringing, education, work, life lived, type of person (happy, strict, giving, caring, community minded, religious...)?

What is his mom's (your grandmother's) story—when and where born, upbringing, education, work, life lived, type of person (happy, strict, giving, caring, community minded, religious…)?

Where does his dad (your grandfather) fit in the lineup of children—first, middle, last, fifth…?

Where does his mom (your grandmother) fit in the lineup of children—first, middle, last, fifth…?

Did your dad know his aunts and uncles (your great aunts and uncles)?

What were his dad's (your grandfather) responsibilities regarding his family growing up? (i.e. babysitter, wood chopper, cleaning, etc.)

What were his mom's (your grandmother) responsibilities regarding her family growing up? (i.e. babysitter, clothes washer, cook, etc.)

Does your dad know much about his parents' (your grandparents) upbringing? Did they enjoy spending time with their parents (your great grandparents)? Siblings (great aunts and uncles)?

What were meals like in their homes? What did they usually eat? Who cooked? Who cleaned up? Where did they eat? Were there any rituals they did?

What was it like in the house his parents' (your grandparents) grew up in?

What was it like in the neighborhood his parents' (your grandparents) grew up in?

Did your dad know his grandparents? What does he know about them?

Did your dad know his great aunts and uncles? What does he know about them?

Did your parents have siblings (do you have aunts and uncles)? If yes, who were they? Did he get along with them? Who did he like? Not like? Do you know your aunts and uncles?

How would your dad describe his siblings—happy, strict, quiet, smart, practical, loving, giving, caring, community minded, reclusive, hard working...?

Notes/Stories

Notes/Stories

Notes/Stories

15
SCHOOL/EDUCATION

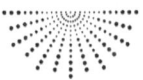

What was his Education?

Today we don't think much about getting an education, at least primary and secondary (elementary to high school) and even on to post secondary (university, college, trades) but in your dad's day it wasn't always the case. Sometimes the school was too far away, sometimes the kids had to be boarded with another family, sometimes correspondence was used but there wasn't always the help to get through the schoolwork, and there wasn't always the belief that education was important, but most boys did attend school. Often though boys or young men were or had to go to work to help feed the family. Find out what things were like when your dad was a child—what were there expectations for him to be educated (was there a certain grade he was expected to go to, was there a certain field he was expected to go into, to excel at...) were his parents educated... what were some of the things he loved about school... what were some of the issues he came up against...

Did your dad go to school?

If yes, when did your dad start school?

Where did he go to school? Was it very far away? Or by correspondence?

How did he get to school?

What did he like about school? What did he dislike about school?

Highest grade he went to? If he didn't finish school, why not?

Favorite subject in elementary? Why?

Favorite subject in junior high? Why?

Favorite subject in high school? Why?

Least favorite subject in elementary? Why?

Least favorite subject in junior high? Why?

Least favorite subject in high school? Why?

His favorite teacher? Why?

His least favorite teacher? Why?

His best friend in elementary? How did they meet?

What things did they do together?

His best friend in junior high? How did they meet?

What things did they do together?

His best friend in high school? How did they meet? What things did they do together?

Did he ever get into trouble at school? Why? What happened?

Did he do any extra-curricular activities? Sports? Music? Art? Was it his choice?

Does he still do any of the activities he learned while growing up, today?

Was he encouraged to go to school? To do well in school? Did that change as he got into higher grades?

How important does he feel that high school education is?

Were there any school dances? Or events?

What did he have for books? Pens/pencils and paper?

Was there lots of homework?

Post Secondary/Trades/Training

Did he go on to post secondary? Trades? Or further training?

Was he supported by his parents? Teachers?

Community? Siblings?

How did he pay for it?

What did he take? Where did he have to go? Was it close or far away? Did he make it home often or see his family often?

Did he like what he took? Did he graduate from it?

How important does he feel that further education—post secondary, trades, training...—is?

Other

What did he want for you in regard to education?

How did his parents feel about education? Were they educated?

Notes/Stories

Notes/Stores

Notes/Stories

16
MARRIAGE/RELATIONSHIPS

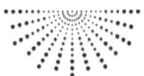

How people meet and get married is often quite fascinating. Sometimes they've known each other since babies, sometimes it's by chance that they meet and sometimes there is quite a story as to how they met. Through the years, the process of meeting and getting married has changed somewhat. In the past, some women and men fell in love and chose to get married, some were told to get married and for some it was arranged for them. Do you know the story of how your parents met? How they fell in love... How the proposal came about... Where they got married... Did they stay married... You might find out some interesting information. You can also ask your dad about his parents and their relationship and how it came about. And do you know the story of your dad's parents?

His Parents

How did his parents meet? How old were they?

What attracted his mom to his dad? Was it an arranged marriage? Or by choice?

How long did they date before getting married?

What was their courtship like?

What kind of work did his father do when they met?

Did his work/career change at all over the years?

How did the marriage proposal happen?

When did they get married? What date? What age were they when they got married?

Where did they get married?

When did they decide to have children?

How many children did they have (how many siblings did your dad have)?

What is a special memory of their relationship?

Did they stay married? Why? Or why not? How long were they married?

Your Parents

How did your parents meet? How old were they?

What attracted your dad to your mom? How long did they date before getting married? What was their courtship like? Was it an arranged marriage?

Was it love at first sight?

How did his parents feel about their relationship?

How did her parents feel about their relationship?

What kind of work did your father do when they met? Did his work/career, change at all over the years?

How did the marriage proposal happen?

When did they get married? What date? How old were they when they got married?

Where did they get married?

What did he want for a wedding day? Did he wear a tux? A suit?

Did he get a wedding ring? Or any symbol of the marriage? Did he wear it?

When did they decide to have children?

How many children did they have (how many siblings do you have)?

What is a special memory of their relationship?

Did they stay married? Why? Or why not? How long were they or have they been married?

What were and are your dad's beliefs about marriage?

What does your dad think is key to a successful marriage?

What did he want for you for marriage and family?

Notes/Stories

Notes/Stories

Notes/Stories

Notes/Stories

17
CAREER/WORK/JOBS

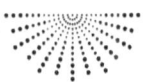

Understanding his work/career/volunteering, is an important conversation because he may not have had a choice as to the type of work he did or the direction his career went. It may have been determined by where he lived, what work was available and the education or training that was available and that he could afford. Volunteering was seen differently and was often something that was encouraged and to some degree was expected.

What did your dad do for work?

Did he ever change jobs?

How old was he when he started working? What was his first job?

How did he feel about the work he did? Did he have a choice of where to work?

What were his responsibilities at work?

Did he move up the chain of responsibility at work?

What did he enjoy about his job?

What did he enjoy least about his job?

Who was the best boss he ever had? What made them good?

Who was the worst boss he ever had? What made them the worst?

What's a job he would have loved to have done but never did?

Did he follow in his dad's footsteps?

What were the expectations of him for work? Was there a specific career he was to go into?

Your Career

What did he want for you for work or a career?

What did he want for your siblings for work or a career?

Notes/Stories

Notes/Stories

Notes/Stories

18
HEALTH

Your health is something that is so important but how to take care of it has changed a fair bit over the years. There are a lot of ideas out there on how best to look after yourself and when you go back in time, there was a lot less use and emphasis on the medical system, people took care of their own health care—some did it well and some not so well. When your dad was young, things were probably done very differently than now. There might have been limited access to any medical health care, there might not have been a hospital nearby and there might not have been a doctor in the area. So what did your dad do for his health?

His Health

What did he do to keep healthy? Did he do things that were considered healthy?

How has his health been throughout his life? (as a child? Teen? in his 20s? 30s? 40s? 50s? 60s? 70s? 80s? 90s?)

Any diseases? Illnesses? Injuries?

If yes, when? How did it come about? How was it treated?

What were some remedies that his parents used when he was a child?

Did he ever have a real scare with his health?

What worked best for him in looking after his health?

Was there ever a remedy that he believed helped him when sick? If yes what was it?

What is his best advice on how to take care of your health?

When did he first go to a doctor? Did he follow what the doctor said?

Your Health (you or your siblings)

How did he handle when you or your siblings got sick as kids? Was he ever involved in looking after you?

Did you or your siblings ever get really sick? Injured? Was there anything special he had to do because of your or your siblings health?

Notes/Stories

Notes/Stories

Notes/Stories

Notes/Stories

Notes/Stories

19
WEALTH

Money is something that men generally have been in charge of their whole lives, so they are a lot more familiar with it than women of their time tend to be. However, money is one of those things that not too many really know how to manage or have a clue how to put it away for the future. Some men did well with using the money they earned to look after themselves and their family, some spent more on themselves than their family and others were just not good with money at all.

What was he taught about money? What did he learn by seeing how his father handled money?

What were his thoughts about money when he was a child? Teenager? Adult? How have his thoughts about money changed over the years?

Did he grow up with money?

Has money always been a struggle? Or has it come easily?

How old was he when he first got paid for work he'd done? Or a job?

Does he feel he was paid fairly for his jobs/career?

What is his advice about money?

Notes/Stories

Notes/Stories

20
TRAVEL

*D*eciding to take a trip today is no big deal. It is really quite easy—you hop in your car and drive to where you want to go or you go online and with a few clicks you've booked and paid for your trip and have your tickets. This has changed a lot over the years and continues to change. The how, when, where and the convenience of booking our travel is so much easier, more convenient and faster, never mind the methods of traveling. We can pretty much travel to anywhere in the world without too much difficulty.

Did he ever travel? As a child? Teen? On his own? With his parents? Siblings? With a friend? With his spouse? With you, his children?

Where did he travel to? Has he ever traveled far from home? Out of his own state/province? Country? Continent?

Did he ever have to travel for work? If yes, to where? Why? How often?

How did he travel? What did it cost?

What place did he love the most?

Where would he love to go back to?

What place did he not enjoy?

Did he ever have a crazy experience while traveling? Where was he going? What happened?

What are the different ways in which he has traveled in his lifetime? i.e. horse, on foot, train, horse and wagon, boat, bus, plane, car, tractor, truck...

What is the most unique way he ever traveled (i.e. horse and buggy, camel, small airplane, etc.)?

Did he ever drive on any of his trips?

What was the neatest thing he ever learned? What was the oddest thing he ever learned?

Who was the most memorable person he met from his travels?

What types of food has he tried? What were his favorites? What were things he didn't like? What was the oddest thing he ever ate?

Did he ever get sick or injured while traveling? What happened? How was it treated?

Did he ever have to end a trip early? Why?

Did he ever go camping? Where? With whom? How did he camp—built his own shelter, cabin, tent, trailer...?

Was he ever caught up in any historical events?

What is his favorite memory of the places he's been to?

Is there one place he thinks you should travel to?

Notes/Stories

Notes/Stories

Notes/Stories

21
BELIEFS

The way we see and understand the world and ourselves really makes all the difference for where we go, what we do and where we end up. Our beliefs direct our lives often in ways we don't understand. Our beliefs are changing and being challenged all the time.

How did your dad see the world as a child? Tween? Teen? In his 20s? 30s? 40s? 50s? 60s? 70s? 80s? 90s? 100's?

What are the things he remembers about how he thought life would be?

What did he believe his life would look like?

What are the beliefs he has held about himself his whole life (good and bad)?

What are the beliefs he struggled with as a teen? In his 20s? 30s? 40s? 50s? 60s? 70s? 80s? 90s? 100s?

How did he handle change? What are some major changes he made in his life? Why? How did they turn out?

How does he think his beliefs have directed his life?

What was his biggest fear about his life?

What does he believe is his greatest accomplishment?

Notes/Stories

Notes/Stories

22
DREAMS/ASPIRATIONS/GOALS

Your dad has or had dreams and aspirations. This is where you get to discover what he wanted in his life and whether he achieved them, made strides toward achieving them or just kept them to himself.

As a little boy, what did he want to be when he grew up?

Did he do it?

If he did was it what he thought it would be?

If not, why not?

What did he do instead?

What are some of the dreams he had? As a teenager? In his 20s? 30s? 40s? 50s? 60s? 70s? 80s? 90s? 100s? Did he achieve any of them?

If he did work towards living his dream, what were some of the problems or issues he encountered along the way?

If he didn't live some of his dreams or reach some of his goals, what does he believe kept him from achieving them?

What does he now see differently that he wished he'd known earlier in life?

What is his biggest achievement?

What is his biggest regret? What does he wish he had done? Or done differently?

What is his greatest learning?

What is he most proud of in his life?

What advice would he give young men of today about work? About family? About life?

What is he happiest about in his life?

Notes/Stories

Notes/Stories

Notes/Stories

Notes/Stories

FAVORITE THINGS TO DO: HOBBIES, SPORTS, MUSIC, ART, WRITING, DANCING...

We all have hobbies, sports, music, artistic endeavors, etc. that we enjoy. Sometimes we continue to do them throughout life but sometimes we don't. Sometimes we stop doing one activity and start a new one. What we do or enjoy often changes over time. Now you can discover what were some things your dad used to do, why he did them and if he continued or quit doing them. Do you know if he was involved in any clubs or held any memberships?

What was his favorite hobby or activity to do as a child? As a teen? 20s? 30s? 40s? 50s? 60s? 70s? 80s? 90s? 100s?

Who taught him?

What was his favorite sport to do as a child? As a teen? 20s? 30s? 40s? 50s? 60s? 70s? 80s? 90s? 100s? Who taught him?

Did he play an instrument? Who taught him?

If yes, what was his favorite music to play to as a child? As a teen? 20s? 30s? 40s? 50s? 60s? 70s? 80s? 90s? 100s?

What was his favorite music to listen to as a child? As a teen? 20s? 30s? 40s? 50s? 60s? 70s? 80s? 90s? 100s?

What were his favorite type of arts, crafts or hobbies to do as a child? As a teen? 20s? 30s? 40s? 50s? 60s? 70s? 80s? 90s? 100s?

What was his creative talent? Did he ever paint? Write? Dance? Sculpt? Other? If yes, who taught him?

What is something he has done that shocked people? When did he do it? Why?

Who did he like to do activities with as a child? Tween? Teen? 20s? 30s? 40s? 50s? 60s? 70s? 80s? 90s? 100s?

Was he ever part of a club? If yes, what was the club and what did they do? How did he become involved with this group?

Did he hold any memberships? If yes, to what? Why did he join?

Did he play games as a child? Adult? What was his favorite game? Board game?

Did he spend much time in nature? Outdoors? What did he like to do outdoors?

As a child, where was his favorite place to hang out? With whom? As a teenager? Young adult? Adult?

Notes/Stories

Notes/Stories

Notes/Stories

24
RAISING YOU

*O*ften we don't ask questions about how we came to be. Sometimes we hear different stories throughout our life about this but we never really ask in a moment of good rapport and not when it is in relation to the current situation. Why does that matter? Because too often, especially in families, things are said at sensitive times or when emotions are high and then they become misunderstood. They can become that pain that we continue to take with us through our lives. It is important to understand that your dad was a man, a human. He did some things really well but some things he didn't do that well. He made some mistakes. Those things he did in life that have stuck with you as a negative, he didn't do to hurt you. It might have been because that was what he'd been taught, what was expected or maybe he was just reacting.

I don't know much about my dad's life as a child and sadly, he's no longer here for me to ask. I know roughly 5 things about his childhood that were really meaningful and gave insight to his life as a child. He used to tell some stories, usually when we were doing something or at an event and he'd say something like, 'we used to...'. It told me at least a bit about how things were but not about him or his life. I think he really struggled with sharing it. Was it guilt? Shame? Or did he just never learn to talk about himself? Was it seen as not acceptable? Maybe weak? I don't know but I do know he had a great sense of humor that he didn't let out enough. That he was very skilled, a hard-worker, very community minded and a good problem solver.

Life was very different back when he was born in the first 1/3 of the 1900s. At age of 12 he was basically running the farm and stepped into the role of the man. He was looking after the family, ensuring they were fed and clothed. He also walked to school really early every day as it was his responsibility to chop wood and heat the schoolhouse for the day before everyone got there. A lot of demands on a young boy. So not only did he have the responsibility of ensuring that his parents and siblings were fed, clothed and sheltered, then when he was in his 20s he had to do that for his own family. Something he'd been doing since he was a boy. It wasn't a question of would he or wouldn't he, it was just things that had to be done and he was the oldest.

I think that having that harsh of an expectation at such a young age and having no real say had to be difficult. But that was the times. At a young age, men were expected to work hard, do the physical labor that was needed and to be responsible. There wasn't always a lot or any time for play or fun. That was a bit too frivolous. Don't get me wrong there were some fun things that happened but it was always second to the hard work and was only if you had the energy to do it.

Does that mean he didn't love me? No. It means he did what he knew and what he thought would raise good, law-abiding, hard-working children. And don't forget he was also trying to deal with his own identity of who he was and what he really wanted. Most of our dads, our elderly dads grew up in a harsh time and most did not see any affection, any love. It was strictly work hard, do what you're told, stay out of trouble and take care of family and community. It doesn't matter who you are, how tough you are, it is something as humans that we all crave—knowing we are loved and that we matter. I'm not sure that all Dads were clear on that.

He was scared that he didn't and couldn't relate to his children. Now I could have held onto the fact that he was a hard man at times and made us work hard as well, made us feel like we weren't all that important except as hard workers. But he did teach us some valuable lessons—how to work hard, how to get things done, to appreciate nature, to appreciate all that we have. He raised kids in a time that you didn't really talk about your personal struggles with being a Dad... With how difficult you found it... The things that went well... The things that didn't go well.... You really kept a lot of that to yourself. And I think that is true for today. We may share some of the things we've found that work but we really don't talk about feeling scared that we're messing up and really aren't sure what we are doing. It is not an easy role in life but it is and can be one of the most rewarding.

To me it was important to understand my dad. I had an interesting connection with my father. It's not something I can explain, it was just there. I always felt there was a deeper connection or maybe it was those moments when he opened himself to be softer and more vulnerable that I felt I got to see some of the man he truly was. I had some amazing conversations with him about being a parent, about things they did with us as kids, about some of my fears, confusion, anxiety. I was at an age and stage when I was finally in a place that I could relate to what he was saying and not take it personally. Raising kids is work, and it means as a Dad, you had a tough role to fill... literally. Many Dads thought they had to be tough to get the kids to do what he thought was going to make them people of good character. And when we are talking about raising kids, 30-40-50+ years ago, you are giving up so much time, energy, and dreams to raise them. My dad always wanted kids but I think like all of us, he struggled with finding himself and in trying to fill that role of Dad, at the same time. I know that he loved us deeply and wanted so much for us, he just often didn't know how to show us or tell us. He often didn't know how to share of himself. He truly was about community though, being involved and making sure that others were taken care of. He was involved in many committees, boards and events in the community his whole life. It was very important to him.

Talk to your dad, not when things are happening but when there is a quiet moment and when you are in rapport with him. Go with an open mind and listen as though listening to someone you don't know. Because in all honesty I bet you may not really know the man you call Dad. Don't take offense to what he says. Just listen and try to get the context of the times. I know for my father, he found a way to go to College. He came from a family that did not encourage that and definitely did not have the money for it but he found a way. Pretty impressive to me.

Expecting You

How did your dad feel about it when your mom was pregnant with you? Your siblings? Any complications? Did your mom being pregnant scare him? Did it scare him being a father?

What was your birth like? Your siblings? Any complications? Where were you born? Where were your siblings born?

How did your parents choose your name? Your siblings' names?

Was your dad able to be present in the room when you were born? Or anyone else? Where was your dad when you were born? What his role, if any, in your or your sibling's birth?

What kind of medical/birthing support was there? What was needed? Or used when you or your siblings were born?

After you were born, did your dad ever carry you around?

Did they have car seats for you?

Was your dad ever involved in feeding you? Bathing you? Putting you to bed?

Raising You

What were his goals for you? How did he see you as a child? What were his hopes and dreams for you? For your siblings?

What are things he wished he had done differently in raising you?

What does he now know that he wished he'd known then?

What is his biggest realization about raising you? Your siblings?

What did he realize about each of you? Was it very different to raise each one of you?

What is one thing available today that he wished he had back then?

What was and is the best part of being a Dad?

What were some of the things he used to make for you (i.e. toys, maybe furniture...)?

What did he tell you about the opposite sex? What did he tell you about dating? Marriage? What did he want for you in regard to a relationship? Children?

What were some fun things you used to do together? What did he love doing with you?

What did he enjoy teaching you?

What did he feel it was important for you to know? How did he feel it was important to show up?

What is he proudest of in raising you?

What did he want for you, in regard to education?

What did he want for you in life?

What did he want you to know about money?

Your Health (you or your siblings)

Was he involved in taking care of you when you got sick? What were some things he did in looking after your health as a child? i.e. when you got the flu, what did he do to treat it?

Did you or your siblings ever get really sick? Injured? Were any of you sick very much?

Your Career

What did he want for you for work or a career? Did he feel it was important?

What did he want for your siblings for work or a career?

Other

Did you ever have pets when you were young? Did he like having pets around?

What is he happiest about with raising you and your siblings?

What are all of your siblings' full names and ages?

Did your family ever attend a special event—show, concert... together?

Did your family ever have family get-togethers or family reunions? If yes, who'd all attend? Was it immediate family? Or extended family? How often? Do they still occur?

Did they ever have neighborhood/community get-togethers? Or picnics?

Notes/Stories

Notes/Stories

Notes/Stories

Notes/Stories

Notes/Stories

25
TOUGH TIMES

We all go through a lot in our lifetime, some things are easy, some are fun, some just happen but some of the things that happen just aren't all that easy to get through. In our lifetime we deal with issues in all areas of our lives from health, money, beliefs about ourselves, to relationships to death. Just imagine how much your dad has seen in his lifetime. He has seen and been through a lot. Are you aware of what many of those issues would be? If your dad is older, odds are that he was involved in one or a few wars. He may or may not want to talk about it. To start, try to ask questions that aren't directly related to what his duties were or what he might have seen. Ask about the food, what did they eat? What were some of the places he was stationed? If you see some military guns or equipment, you might ask if he ever saw any of that. This can be a really tough subject; you will need to determine if he is ready or able to talk about it and if you're ready to hear it. It can be very emotional for him and can be for you as well. Understand and respect that he just might not be able to.

What were some tough things he had to deal with in his life (family, health, marriage, children, aging, community, friends, relatives, housing/accommodations, loss of loved ones, loss of something...)? As a child? Tween? Teen? In his 20s? 30s? 40s? 50s? 60s? 70s? 80s? 90s? 100s?

How did he handle the situations? How does he think it changed his moving forward? What did he learn to believe from that situation? How did others see those situations?

What kept him moving forward?

Did he ever struggle with putting enough food on the table? With ensuring you, his kids, had what they needed?

What is his advice for getting through tough situations?

Was he involved in any wars? If yes, in what respect? Is he willing to talk to you about it?

Notes/Stories

Notes/Stories

Notes/Stories

Notes/Stories

26
FRIENDS

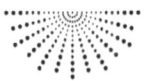

Through our lifetime we meet many people. Your dad has probably met a lot of people throughout his life. Some will have left a lasting impression, some positive and some not so positive. Some of those he has met will have become casual friends while others will have become good friends. Who were some of those people who have passed through your dad's life? Who were those people who had a positive impact on him? The thing about friends is they are there for the good and the bad, the fun and the sad.

Who was his best friend as a child? Teen? 20s? 30s? 40s? 50s? 60s? 70s? 80s? 90s? 100s?

How did he and his best friend meet?

What were some things he and his best friend used to do? To talk about?

Did your dad have anyone that he did sports with? That he worked with? That he talked with? That he did hobbies with, i.e. fishing?

Who were some of his friends, throughout his life? How did he meet them? What were things they liked to do?

Has he kept in touch with any of his friends over the years?

Are any of his friends still alive?

Who did he talk to when he had problems? As a child? Teen? 20s? 30s? 40s? 50s? 60s? 70s? 80s? 90s? 100s? Or did he talk to anyone?

Did he ever have any pen-pals? Who? How long did he stay in touch? Did they ever meet in person?

Did he find it easy or hard to make friends throughout his life?

Who are some of his friends now? What do they like to do together?

What does being a friend mean to him?

Notes/Stories

Notes/Stories

27
RELIGION/SPIRITUALITY

This is another area many say not to have a conversation about but it can be quite interesting to know what your dad's views are on religion and spirituality —what was he taught as a child? what was he raised to believe? and how or if that has changed over time?

Was he raised in a religious or spiritual household?

What were some of their religious or spiritual practices?

What is his belief about religion? About spirituality? Has that changed over the years?

What are his religious or spiritual practices today?

What did he feel was important that you, his children understood about religion or spirituality when you were young? Now?

What is important to him about religion? Spirituality?

When he dies what does he believe will happen to him?

What does he want for a funeral?

Notes/Stories

Notes/Stories

28
POLITICS

Politics is often another subject many want to stay away from, however it would be good to know your dad's view on this topic. Do not let this be something that divides you, though.

What were his political views growing up? Now?

What does he think of the politics of today?

Does he vote? Why or why not?

Does he see voting as important? Why? Or why not?

Was he ever involved in politics?

What does he want you to know about politics?

Did he ever get into arguments over politics?

Who does he believe is the best leader in politics that he has seen in his lifetime?

Does he think you should be more involved in politics and what is going on?

Notes/Stories

Notes/Stories

THE MOST HELPFUL THINGS YOU LEARNED FROM DAD

This is a list of the things that you and your siblings have learned from him that has helped you the most.

His Advice

What are those things he used to tell you, those things you heard but maybe took for granted or kind of brushed off as I've heard this before, or yeah, I get it... but now you realize how wise they were... how fun they were... how eye opening they were...

This is a list of the things you and your siblings have learned from your dad that has helped you the most. Those words of wisdom, funny things he used to say, how he approached certain situations, the positive way he treated people... All those neat things he either taught you or he demonstrated through who he was and is.

What were his words of wisdom?

How did he approach stressful situations?

How did he approach difficult situations?

How did he approach people in general?

How did he approach difficult people?

What was something funny he used to say?

What was some neat things he used to do for others?

About Life

What is his best advice about life?

Being happy

What does he believe makes him happy? What does he believe would keep you happy?

Dreams/Goals

What is his best advice about going for your dreams and goals?

Education

What is his advice about getting further education?

Career

What was his view or expectation for a career for you?

Relationships

What makes a good relationship? How do you keep a good relationship?

Family

What is his advice about family? What does it take to make a family happy? The best way to raise kids? The best thing to teach them?

Other

What advice did he always give you growing up?

What did he always say to you growing up?

What was his best advice overall?

What does he feel is the best part about aging?

What is his fondest memory?

What were some of those things that he kept telling you about life as a child? Tween? Teen? Adult?

Notes/Stories

Notes/Stories

Notes/Stories

Notes/Stories

30
FAVORITE HOW TO'S, THINGS HE FIXED, BUILT...

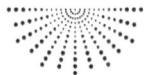

There are those things you may remember your dad building or fixing when you were that makes you always think of Dad—from fixing the household appliances, vehicles, building useful things to use... It's also those fun things he made for you to play with—toys, fixing our bikes, things for a school project... Or the things he used to build or make to use... Or the crafts or hobbies he used to do...

There are so many things our dads teach us, so many things we take for granted. This is a great time and a great place to write down those things he has taught you that you really want to remember and keep for the future.

What were some of his favorite things to tinker with? What were yours? Did you do them together?

What were some of the things he made for you to play with as a child (i.e. toys...)? Tween? Teen? Adult? How did he make them?

What were some of the things he made and used? Or made for you to use?

Did he do wood working...? Was there a pattern that he used to use that you'd like to learn? Or to keep?

Did your dad build things, make things or fix things? How did he do it? What did he use?

What was something he used to make that you used as a child? Tween? Teen? Adult?

How did he make...?

What did he used to do when...?

What inspired him to make...?

Notes/Stories

Notes/Stories

Notes/Stories

Notes/Stories

FAMILY HISTORY AND STORIES

*H*ere you can keep track of family members who they are and you can write down some of the stories about different people you're related to or about your family history.

Who are the people who make up your past? What are some of the stories about those people your dad is always talking about? Do a simple family tree so you remember 'who was who' and how they are related. Also keep track of any information you might want to remember about them.

If you're unsure how to create a family tree, here are some ideas for how to create them and the information you might want to document. How far back in your family history you want to go is up to you. You might also want to include more information about who each of your ancestors were—where they lived, worked and some stories about their lives. Have fun with this.

Format 1:

Grandparents name and date of birth and where born.

Their children's (your dad and your aunts and uncles) names and dates of birth

Their children's (you, your siblings, your cousins) names and dates of birth

Format 2:

Grandparents (names and date of birth)

Their Children (dad and siblings names and dates of birth)

Their Children (You and your cousins' names and dates of birth)

Family Tree

Notes/Stories

32
YOUR MEMORIES

*H*ere you can keep track of the memories you have of your dad, those special moments in your life where he was there for you. Or those cool things you know he did.

What are favorite things he did for you as a child?

Your favorite smell that reminds you of him?

An activity you enjoyed doing together?

A joke between you?

A song you both enjoyed?

A place you liked to visit?

An event you both loved to watch or go to?

Something he did that you hold dear?

Something he said to you that is important to you?

How you see him growing up? Now?

What are some mementos that remind you of your dad? Or a special time?

Is there a time of year or a special occasion that always brings him to mind?

Notes/Stories

Notes/Stories

Notes/Stories

Notes/Stories

33
KEEP THE CONVERSATIONS GOING

The truth is we all go through good times and we all go through hard times at some point or other in our life. The interesting thing about those difficult times is whether you are able to put them in perspective and move on without those things keeping you down, angry or bitter. The best piece of advice I can give is to re-frame those situations and to come from a place of gratitude. Be thankful for every day and every event, find the positive and discover what you can learn from it but don't hold on to the anger. Look for the good, look for what will help you to move forward... and move on. If you are struggling with this, find someone, maybe a mentor, coach, or other professional, who can help you to understand and to re-frame your relationship. It is time to grow, mend and heal.

My hope is that you'll be able to create a stronger, more loving bond but I do know that it is not possible in all cases. For your benefit though, put your Dad and his life into perspective in relationship to yours. He did what he knew with what was really societal norms. It might have been enough but it might not have been. He did not act the way he did to hurt you; he did it because he had been taught that role of a man, of a dad. Love him and forgive him, it will help you to heal.

The key to connecting with your dad, is to meet him where he is at. What are the things that have meaning for him? What are the things that you can connect with him over? As I've mentioned throughout the book, try to find those things he relates to and step into his world. When you can, share your experiences as well.

If your dad is struggling with talking about himself or his life, help him see the good of who he is and all he has done. For some children, it can be difficult to share with their father or to connect with him but if possible, help him to see the positive that has come out of his life. Let him know about all the good things he did for you in your life, all that he taught you, provided for you, made for you, all the things that helped you grow as a person… He is a good man, one who has flaws and quirks and hang-ups like the rest of us. Honor your dad. But also honor yourself, recognize who you are. Know that you can put the past into perspective and re-frame how you see it. Remember this is about moving forward so you can be happy, know you mattered and feel connected and loved. And hopefully you can help your dad achieve that as well.

Use this journey of exploring his history, to understand his and to keep those conversations going.

There are some extra blank pages where you can keep track of the additional stories he tells. It might be about how he came to live where he is... more about his parents... his siblings... his journey... some special moments in his life... some traumatic moments his life... some neat things he learned... how he views the world... any vices he might have had... something he tried for the fun of it...

Notes/Stories

Notes/Stories

Notes/Stories

Notes/Stories

Notes/Stories

Dad

Dad is a mixture

Of strength

Hard work

Teaching us

Fixing things

Responsibility

Community

Mentor

Leader

Guide

He is Dad!

ABOUT THE AUTHOR

Glenna is a multi-award-winning author, speaker and coach and founder of The Women Writes Movement. She writes page-turning suspense/thrillers (Maggie Thom) and she writes heart connecting and humorous nonfiction (Glenna Mageau). Glenna has interviewed many elderly about their lives and their stories. She is truly inspired by their journeys, their knowledge and their wisdom and believes that we need to start these conversations so that their journeys can be told and preserved.

Glenna's latest book—*Do You Know Your Dad's Story? The Unasked Questions.* —is a way to get conversations started between dad and adult child. It is a way to get Dad to share his journey and his life, in particular elderly fathers. Glenna's goal is that when we go into old age, we should feel loved, connected and know our lives mattered. Understanding your dad's journey will help you to understand him in a whole new light.

To learn more: www.glennamageau.com

facebook.com/authorglennamageau
twitter.com/GlennaMageau
pinterest.com/GlennaMageau

OTHER BOOKS BY GLENNA MAGEAU

Do You Know Your Mom's Story? 365 Questions You Need to Ask Her.

"...it reaches far beyond dates of birth, marriage and death and into the heart and soul of a woman and her family..."

— MULTI-AWARD-WINNING AUTHOR P.M. TERRELL

What do you really know about your Mom?

Do you know what her hopes, dreams and desires were? Did she live them?

Your mom is so much more than the woman who raised you. She grew up in a time very different from yours—there were different beliefs, habits, and ways of doing things. Your mom has seen a lot in her life, getting to hear her journey will help you to understand her in a whole new light. Now is the time get to know her and to document her life. The only way to find out about your mom's story is to ask… because one day she won't be there anymore.

When we reach old age we should know our lives mattered, that we mattered, that we are loved, happy and feel connected.

This book offers a way to start conversations between you and your mom—in particular, elderly mothers. It is a guide which provides questions to ask, as well as how and when to ask them. Use this as a way to grow, heal and/or mend the relationship between mom and child; preserve this woman's journey through life and in particular her role as Mom. Her story is her legacy to you.

> *"…insightful questions with thought provoking examples and explanations…"*
>
> — CHRISTINE JACKSON

More Books by Glenna Mageau

Nonfiction

Don't Laugh: A Woman's Playbook to the U-R In Line for the Women's Public Bathroom Again!

Fiction - Suspense/Thrillers (under the penname Maggie Thom)

The Caspian Wine Series
Captured Lies
Deceitful Truths
Split Seconds

Other Suspense/Thriller Fiction

Tainted Waters
Deadly Ties

Thank You for Reading

Do You Know Your Dad's Story? The Unasked Questions

I hope you enjoyed reading it as much as I enjoyed writing it.

Please leave a review on the online bookstores, it helps others to find it.

Recommend this book to family and friends, coworkers, women and men everywhere—help them to document their dad's life and hopefully to also grow, mend or heal their relationships with their dad's.

I'd love to hear from you, how you are finding connecting with your dad, what you've learned and anything about this journey that you'd like to share. And if you come up with more questions to ask your dad I'd love to hear them.

Email me at author@glennamageau.com

Website: www.glennamageau.com

www.ingramcontent.com/pod-product-compliance
Lightning Source LLC
Chambersburg PA
CBHW030905080526
44589CB00010B/153